Montana
wild and beautiful

Photography by Chuck Haney and John Reddy

MONTANA
MAGAZINE

American & World Geographic Publishing

Front cover: Red paintbrush and yellow buttercups herald summer along Picnic Creek below Mount Aeneas in the Swan Range.
CHUCK HANEY PHOTO

Back cover: Big Hole haystacks, Bitterroot Mountains on the horizon.
JOHN REDDY PHOTO

Title page: Autumn gold in the Yaak.
JOHN REDDY PHOTO

Right: Glacial ice-water pours down Hole-in-the-Wall, Glacier National Park.
JOHN REDDY PHOTO

© 1999 American & World Geographic Publishing
Photographs as marked © 1999 Chuck Haney
Photographs as marked © 1999 John Reddy

This book may not be reproduced in whole or in part by any means (with the exception of short quotes for the purpose of review) without permission of the publisher. For more information on our books call or write: American & World Geographic Publishing, P.O. Box 5630, Helena, MT 59604, (406) 443-2842 or (800) 654-1105, or visit our website: www.montanamagazine.com

Printed in Singapore

Chuck Haney

My portion of the book is dedicated to all those who have been so supportive and helpful to my photography pursuits: to my late grandparents Urban and Elvera Thieroff, who gave me hope and made me into the man I am; to my wife Diana, who has supported my dreams from day one, and keeps our home running while I'm on the road—I love you; to my biggest fan, my mother Janice, and to my late father, Billy Haney—my spirt is with you daily.

—C.H.

Bighorn sheep, alert on Mount Wilbur, Glacier National Park.
CHUCK HANEY PHOTO

It's said there is a story behind every picture.

The warmth of a tent woodstove invites me inside to join my camping buddies. Lively banter competes with the crackling of cottonwood shards and flows as freely as the cowboy coffee while the prospect of exploring a nearby canyon excites everyone. I've already hiked above the bottomland and captured the day's first light against the cream-colored cliffs of the Missouri River. A crisp October morning and we are alone with the mighty river. On this morning, life in Montana is really good.

The images you are about to view have been gleaned from a literal mountain of 35mm and medium-format transparencies shot over the last few seasons. These are the successes and triumphs. Finding great Montana subjects is easy. Producing publishable images is a lot of hard work. Mosquitos, muddy roads and the sweat of lugging heavy packs across mountainous terrain make the effort challenging. For all the great images there are many times of high clouds and flat light that leave me waiting until next year's visit.

I must admit that I never need an alarm clock to roll out of bed when shooting. I'm probably much more enthusiastic at 4 a.m. than any other time, especially when Mother Nature greets the day with those golden moments of light that happen only once in a while. I admit it, I'm addicted to fleeting moments of magical light.

I've pedaled my bicycle across prairie plains that once felt the thunder of a million or more bison hooves. Climbed mountain peaks that held visions for native peoples. I've dipped a paddle along the White Cliffs of the Missouri River where the Lewis and Clark party explored nearly two centuries ago. Being in these places brings me into focus, helps me capture the spirit of this amazing land. When the light gets good, I don't think about my next move; a natural instinct takes over. These are the times that produce the best images.

Montanans have always regarded the land in an almost spiritual context. Places such as the Rocky Mountain Front, the White Cliffs of the Missouri, and badlands of Makoshika State Park rewind our consciousness to the past while reminding us of how valued they will be for our future. Montana is a land worth preserving.

Throughout my travels across Montana, it's the people I meet that leave the most lasting memories. Friendly conversations are struck up over ham and eggs and the local newspaper at cafes, ranchers and farmers invite me in for coffee, and hikers and bikers share infectious appetites for the beauty that unfolds along their paths. I've made friends for life by traveling the Montana road. In fact, I've never met anyone who didn't like Montana. Montanans are a special breed. My photography work takes me from the Great Plains to the Pacific Ocean. Whenever I meet someone who has noticed my 7P Montana license plates, I'm quite sure they hear the homeland pride in my voice. There is nowhere else on earth quite like Montana, and I long to see as much of it as possible.

I hope you enjoy my photographic journey. If my images accurately represent the Treasure State, then I've done my job. If my photographs move you, then I've fulfilled my calling.

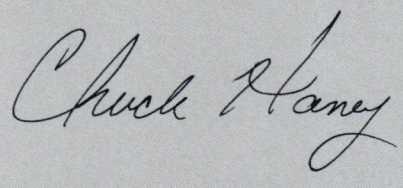

A foggy dawn on Yellowstone National Park's Madison River.
CHUCK HANEY PHOTO

A touch of autumn in the air along Ross Creek in extreme northwestern Montana.
JOHN REDDY PHOTO

John Reddy

My interest in the outdoors began with family picnics and outings when I was a young boy. I remember climbing around on rocks with my nephews, who are only a few years younger than I, as my dad, mom, sister and brother-in-law watched.

My first extended backpacking trip, at the age of eighteen, was one that probably should have been saved for later, when I had more practical experience. I went with a high school friend, Dan, whose uncle Arnie was a cropduster in Cut Bank. Arnie had offered to fly us in to Schafer Meadows in the Bob Marshall Wilderness. After a near-zero-gravity demonstration of what it feels like to dust crops, we were welcomed at the landing site by an audience consisting of a cow moose and her calf. We watched as Arnie's plane disappeared. With a pair of cheap backpacks, an even cheaper tent, boots that eventually produced bleeding blisters, and a borrowed Smith & Wesson .44 magnum that we had never fired, we were ready for anything! We stayed awake all the first night clutching the massive .44 while a grizzly poked around outside our tent. As day broke we gathered enough courage to leave the tent. It turned out that the noises from the night were a squirrel dropping pine cones on our tent! For the next forty miles we experienced a plethora of conditions and emotions: wetness, cold, heat, sweat, exhaustion, fear, pain, wonder, and elation…it was great!

The photographs from that trip, which I thought were pretty damned good at the time, now serve only as a reminder that I had to start somewhere.

I loved taking pictures so much I decided to study photography at MSU in Bozeman. This, after a failed attempt to become an electrical engineer! Midway through the four-year program I decided to become an "artist." After all, that was the thing to do in the '70s. After endless late-night philosophical arguments about whether photography is "art," and discussions of hidden meanings contained in images, I eventually returned to my roots, photographing nature.

I find myself drawn, photographically, to the smaller, less obvious aspects of the Montana landscape. The panoramic vistas are still important, but the intimacy of working closer is more challenging. Part of that comes from working with a 4x5 field camera where nothing is automatic and the image is dim and upside down. It forces you into a closer relationship with the subject.

Montana has always inspired me. I love how well defined the seasons are: there is never any doubt what time of year it is. I love the cathedral peaks and clear lakes of Glacier. I love the endlessness of the plains. I love the serenity and isolation of the Yaak. I love the quiet openness of the Big Hole. I love the incredible hugeness of the Beartooth. I love the morning fog in the Bitterroot Valley. I love the windswept purity of the Rocky Mountain Front. I love the fact that there are still Montanans who don't know where the awesome Centennial Valley is. I truly love it all!

I admire and respect the struggling farmers and ranchers who have been the stewards of the land, and I envy their sweat-and-dirt connection to it. They are the salt of the earth.

As I get older, I sometimes feel an urgency to see all there is to see in Montana before it's too late. Of course that isn't possible. I won't regret not seeing it all: I'm grateful to have seen as much as I have.

John Reddy

I dedicate my pictures here to my Dad, who didn't live long enough to see his grandson, and to my son Joe who, I hope, will someday know the wonders of being a father.

—J.R.

Traditional Montana sign-decorating near Denton.
JOHN REDDY PHOTO

Above: National Park Service barn, with Bad Marriage Mountain on the horizon, Glacier National Park.
CHUCK HANEY PHOTO

Facing page: Kootenai River Falls near Libby.
JOHN REDDY PHOTO

Left: Chilly reflection in the Middle Fork of the Flathead River, Glacier National Park.
JOHN REDDY PHOTO

Below: Forty winks for a Yellowstone National Park coyote.
CHUCK HANEY PHOTO

Above: Built to last at Laurin, near Virginia City.
JOHN REDDY PHOTO

Facing page: Bear Creek flowing into the Middle Fork of the Flathead River.
CHUCK HANEY PHOTO

Above: Glacier National Park's Mahtotopa Mountain greets the new day.
CHUCK HANEY PHOTO

Right: Fat tires take on the Moiese Hills above the Flathead River.
CHUCK HANEY PHOTO

Above: Sundown symphony in the Big Hole.
JOHN REDDY PHOTO

Facing page: West Fork of the Bull River flowing below the Cabinet Mountains.
JOHN REDDY PHOTO

A field of arrowleaf balsamroot in front of the Rocky Mountain Front.
JOHN REDDY PHOTO

Above: Lodgepole pines lost in the fog.
JOHN REDDY PHOTO

Right: "Prairie smoke" or "old man's whiskers," this plant is well named.
CHUCK HANEY PHOTO

Facing page: Mission Valley wheat ranch.
CHUCK HANEY PHOTO

Right: Little Bighorn River near Lodge Grass.
CHUCK HANEY PHOTO

Below: To go or to stay? A mule deer on the Rocky Mountain Front.
CHUCK HANEY PHOTO

Above: Flathead Lake "gems."
JOHN REDDY PHOTO

Right: Canada goose.
JOHN REDDY PHOTO

Facing page: Handy storage for life's necessities, in the Blackfoot River Valley.
JOHN REDDY PHOTO

Above: Exploring Otokomi Mountain high in Glacier National Park.
CHUCK HANEY PHOTO

Facing page: Sacred Dancing Cascade on McDonald Creek, Glacier National Park.
JOHN REDDY PHOTO

Above: Geese on Summit Lake in the Swan Valley.
JOHN REDDY PHOTO

Facing page: The weather is closing in on Mount Clements, Glacier National Park.
JOHN REDDY PHOTO

Above: On Hailstone National Wildlife Refuge, near Rapelje.
CHUCK HANEY PHOTO

Left: Decision Point, where the Marias River meets the Missouri.
CHUCK HANEY PHOTO

Summer storm in the Absaroka Range near Livingston.
JOHN REDDY PHOTO

Above: Wind sculpture in the Terry Badlands.
CHUCK HANEY PHOTO

Right: A newborn elk's bath beside the Gardiner River, Yellowstone National Park.
CHUCK HANEY PHOTO

Facing page: In Mount Haggin Wildlife Management Area, between Anaconda and Wisdom, the Mule Ranch is part of an area set aside for summer and winter sports amid the Pintler Range.
JOHN REDDY PHOTO

Above: Morrell Falls in the Swan Valley.
JOHN REDDY PHOTO

Facing page: Clouds lifting in Glacier National Park.
JOHN REDDY PHOTO

Preceding pages: Sandstone formations in today's Wild and Scenic portion of the Missouri River struck Meriwether Lewis, in 1805, as like "elegant ranges of…buildings, having their parapets well stocked with statuary."
CHUCK HANEY PHOTO

Above: Calves on the Hargrave Ranch near Marion.
CHUCK HANEY PHOTO

Right: A Belgian draft horse ready for work in the Belt area.
JOHN REDDY PHOTO

Far right: Cool nights and crisp days at Lower St. Mary Lake, Glacier National Park.
JOHN REDDY PHOTO

Restless spirits above Little Bighorn Battlefield National Monument.
CHUCK HANEY PHOTO

Trucks by summer, and snowmobiles by winter: Cooke City, an entrance to Yellowstone National Park.
CHUCK HANEY PHOTO

Above: Day is done at North American Indian Days, Browning.
CHUCK HANEY PHOTO

Left: Missouri River ice sheets near Fort Benton.
CHUCK HANEY PHOTO

Above: In Yellowstone National Park: Minerva Terrace.
CHUCK HANEY PHOTO

Grand Prismatic Springs (right), and Lower Falls of the Yellowstone River (facing page).
JOHN REDDY PHOTOS

Beargrass below Mount Oberlin and Mount Cannon, Glacier National Park.
JOHN REDDY PHOTO

Quiet pleasures on Little Therriault Lake, near Eureka.
CHUCK HANEY PHOTO

Right: Chalk Buttes in Custer National Forest, extreme southeastern Montana.
JOHN REDDY PHOTO

Below: Pronghorn in Bowdoin National Wildlife Refuge.
CHUCK HANEY PHOTO

Above: Grain elevators in the heart of the Golden Triangle.
CHUCK HANEY PHOTO

Facing page: Refrigerator Canyon, near York, lives up to its name.
JOHN REDDY PHOTO

Above: Cedar in the moist Bitterroot Mountains.
JOHN REDDY PHOTO

Facing page: Looking to Mount Reynolds from Hidden Lake Pass, Glacier National Park.
JOHN REDDY PHOTO

Above: Rainbow Lake in the Beartooth Mountains.
JOHN REDDY PHOTO

Facing page: Aspens in the Two Medicine Valley, Glacier National Park.
JOHN REDDY PHOTO

Left: Wild geraniums near Chief Mountain on a summer dawn.
CHUCK HANEY PHOTO

Below: Heavy Runner Mountain, near Glacier National Park's Logan Pass.
CHUCK HANEY PHOTO

Above: Farmland east of the Rocky Mountain Front.
JOHN REDDY PHOTO

Facing page: Cataract Falls in the Lewis and Clark National Forest on the Rocky Mountain Front.
CHUCK HANEY PHOTO

Following pages: Alpenglow on Blackleaf Canyon, Rocky Mountain Front.
CHUCK HANEY PHOTO

Above: Black angus herd at the Medicine Rocks, near Ekalaka.
CHUCK HANEY PHOTO

Left: Sugarbeets, an important eastern Montana crop, in the Yellowstone River Valley near Sidney.
CHUCK HANEY PHOTO

Below: Lichen-covered rock near Crown Butte, west of Great Falls.
CHUCK HANEY PHOTO

Above: Dressed for fall, near St. Regis.
JOHN REDDY PHOTO

Facing page: An autumn mood on Lake McDonald, Glacier National Park.
JOHN REDDY PHOTO

Right: Yucca growing on Sunshine Ridge above the Wild and Scenic Missouri River.
CHUCK HANEY PHOTO

Below: Time to spread the alarm to the prairie dog town?
CHUCK HANEY PHOTO

Above: Garnet ghost town.
JOHN REDDY PHOTO

Facing page: Day's end at McWenneger Slough near Kalispell.
CHUCK HANEY PHOTO

Preceding pages: Sainfoin, a forage crop, near Bynum.
CHUCK HANEY PHOTO

Above: The spring wheat is up,
near Great Falls.
JOHN REDDY PHOTO

Right: Kayaking past House Rock
on the Gallatin River.
JOHN REDDY PHOTO

Facing page: Cabin Creek
in the Bitterroot Mountains.
JOHN REDDY PHOTO

Above: Autumn mosaic.
JOHN REDDY PHOTO

Left: Aspens in Glacier National Park, near Kiowa.
JOHN REDDY PHOTO

Looking across Bighorn Canyon National Recreation Area to the Pryor Mountains.
JOHN REDDY PHOTO

Above: Purple of lupine, pink of owl clover, white of yarrow, and silvery green of big sage, near Ovando.
JOHN REDDY PHOTO

Right: Rough Lake in the Absaroka-Beartooth Wilderness.
JOHN REDDY PHOTO

Above: Hard at work near Geraldine, below the Highwood Mountains.
JOHN REDDY PHOTO

Left: Jerusalem Rocks near Sweetgrass.
CHUCK HANEY PHOTO

Below: Canada thistle abloom near Kalispell.
CHUCK HANEY PHOTO

Above: Tough traveling in the Bridger Mountain foothills near Bozeman.
JOHN REDDY PHOTO

Facing page: Looking across Holland Lake to the Swan Range.
JOHN REDDY PHOTO

Above: Spring melt swells Elk Creek below the Centennial Mountains.
JOHN REDDY PHOTO

Right: Lodgepole pines in the Little Belt Mountains.
JOHN REDDY PHOTO

Facing page: One way to enjoy the undammed Yellowstone River.
CHUCK HANEY PHOTO

Right: Castle Reef reflected in Pishkun Canal near Choteau.
CHUCK HANEY PHOTO

Below: A field of summer—daisies.
CHUCK HANEY PHOTO

Above: Cottonwoods along the Marias River, Liberty County.
CHUCK HANEY PHOTO

Facing page: Kinney Coulee in Makoshika State Park.
CHUCK HANEY PHOTO

Above: Looking east along Going-to-the-Sun Road, Glacier National Park.
JOHN REDDY PHOTO

Right: Many Glacier Hotel in Glacier National Park is dwarfed by Grinnell Point.
CHUCK HANEY PHOTO

Facing page: Serious travelers on Glacier National Park's St. Mary Bridge.
CHUCK HANEY PHOTO

Above: Flathead Lake sunset.
JOHN REDDY PHOTO

Left: Goodnight to the Whitefish Range in Glacier National Park.
CHUCK HANEY PHOTO

Above: In Freezeout Lake National Wildlife Refuge.
CHUCK HANEY PHOTO

Facing page: Bracken ferns and devil's club on the forest floor.
JOHN REDDY PHOTO

Above: Aspen leaves along the Gallatin River.
JOHN REDDY PHOTO

Facing page: A bison rests beside Soda Butte Creek in Yellowstone National Park.
JOHN REDDY PHOTO

Above: Lucky dairy farm below Columbia Mountain near Whitefish.
CHUCK HANEY PHOTO

Facing page: A moment of wonder among the Ross Creek cedars in northwestern Montana's Bull River Valley.
JOHN REDDY PHOTO

Above: Hay bales between Avon and Elliston, with the Garnet Range on the horizon.
JOHN REDDY PHOTO

Left: Prickly pear cactus blossoms above cottonwood-lined Marias River.
CHUCK HANEY PHOTO

Above: The Boulder River Valley south of Big Timber.
JOHN REDDY PHOTO

Facing page: LaBarge Rock, named for a steamboat captain who often passed by, in the White Cliffs of the Missouri River.
CHUCK HANEY PHOTO

Above: Melville's Lutheran Church, built in 1885, houses Montana's oldest Lutheran congregation.
CHUCK HANEY PHOTO

Left: Canola in bloom in the Mission Valley near Polson.
CHUCK HANEY PHOTO

Preceding pages: Singleshot Mountain above St. Mary Lake, Glacier National Park.
CHUCK HANEY PHOTO

Above: Early autumn morning near Lolo.
JOHN REDDY PHOTO

Facing page: Avalanche Creek Gorge in Glacier National Park.
JOHN REDDY PHOTO

Above: Foxtail barley, Yellowstone National Park.
JOHN REDDY PHOTO

Right: Rocky Mountain Front stock barn near Choteau.
CHUCK HANEY PHOTO

Above: Hi-line grain elevator west of Chester on U.S. Highway 2.
CHUCK HANEY PHOTO

Facing page: The Deer Lodge Valley spreads out below the Flint Creek Range.
JOHN REDDY PHOTO

Above: Prickly pear cactus in flower in the Terry Badlands.
CHUCK HANEY PHOTO

Facing page: The Swan River rolls through Lolo National Forest.
JOHN REDDY PHOTO

Above: Cattle guard on a ranch road near Jordan.
CHUCK HANEY PHOTO

Preceding pages: Lake Mary Ronan, Flathead Lake, and the Mission Mountains.
CHUCK HANEY PHOTO